The
Threshold
of the
Spiritual
World

The
Threshold
of the
Spiritual
World

RUDOLF STEINER

COSIMOCLASSICS

NEW YORK

The Threshold of the Spiritual World
Cover © 2007 Cosimo, Inc.

For information, address:

Cosimo, P.O. Box 416
Old Chelsea Station
New York, NY 10113-0416

or visit our website at:
www.cosimobooks.com

The Threshold of the Spiritual World was originally published in 1918.

Cover design by www.kerndesign.net

ISBN: 978-1-60206-052-4

Spiritual events and beings crowd
in upon man when he has prepared
his soul to perceive them.

——from Chapter II

CONTENTS

The Threshold of the Spiritual World

CONTENTS

Introductory Remarks

IN this book there are given in an aphoristic form some descriptions of those parts of the universe and of the human being which come into view when spiritual knowledge crosses the boundary between the physical and spiritual worlds. It has not been sought to give either a systematic or in any way a complete account, but merely a few descriptions of spiritual experiences, without any fixed plan. In this respect the present work, like my book, *A Road to Self-Knowledge* (published last year), is intended to complete and amplify my other writings. Yet it has also been sought to give the description in such a way that it may be read independently, without any knowledge of these other works.

One who really means to work his way to a knowledge of spiritual science will feel the necessity of contemplating the spiritual side of life from continually fresh points of view. It is indeed only natural that a certain one-sidedness should be connected with every presentation of this kind. This must be the case much more with descriptions of the spiritual spheres than with those of the physical world. And if we rest satisfied with merely one account, we cannot be said to be pursuing spiritual knowledge seriously. My desire, by such writings as this, is to be of use to those who are really in earnest in seeking knowledge of the spiritual world. On this account I try to present spiritual facts again and again from fresh points of view in spite of my having described them from other points of view in other works. Such accounts are complementary of each other, like photographs of a person or an event taken from various points.

In every such description, made from a certain standpoint, there is an opportunity for communicating knowledge which is not attainable from the other points of view. There are again in this book formulae for meditation for those who are seeking spiritual sight for themselves. Those who are looking for such formulae wherewith to develop the life of their soul will find them here.

RUDOLF STEINER.

MUNICH,
August 1913.

The Threshold of the Spiritual World

I

Concerning the Reliance which may be placed on Thinking; the Nature of the Thinking Soul; and of Meditation

IN waking consciousness human thought is like an island in the midst of the stream of the soul's life, which flows by in impressions, sensations, feelings, and so forth. We have to a certain degree finished with an impression or a sensation when we have formed an idea concerning it, that is, when we have framed a thought which throws light on the impression or sensation. Even in a storm of passion and emotion, a certain degree of calm may set in, if the ship of the soul has worked its way to the island of thought.

The soul has a natural confidence in thinking. It feels that if it could not have this confidence, all stability in life would be lost. The healthy life of the soul comes to an end when it begins to doubt about thinking. For even if we cannot arrive at a clear understanding of something through thought, we may yet have the consolation that clearness would result if we could only rouse ourselves to think with sufficient force and exactness. We can reassure ourselves with regard to our own incapacity to clear up a point by thinking; but the thought is intolerable that thinking itself would not be able to bring satisfaction, if we were to penetrate as far into its domain as was necessary for gaining full light on some definite situation in life.

This attitude of the soul with regard to thinking underlies all human efforts after knowledge. It may be dulled in certain moods of the soul, but it is always to be found in the soul's dim feelings. The thinker who doubts the validity and power of thought itself is deceived about the fundamental state of his soul. For it is often really his acuteness of thought which, being overstrained, constructs doubts and perplexities. If he did not really rely on thinking, he would not be tormented with these doubts, which after all are only the result of thinking.

One who develops in himself the feeling here indicated with regard to thought, feels that the latter is not merely something which he is cultivating in himself as a human force of the soul, but also something which quite independently of him and his soul bears within itself some Being of a cosmic nature, a cosmic Being to whom he must work his way, if he intends to live in something which belongs at the same time to him and to the world that is independent of him.

There is something deeply tranquillising in being able to surrender oneself to the life of thought. The soul feels that in that life it can escape from itself.

10

This feeling is as necessary to the soul as the opposite one of being able to be wholly within itself.

In the necessary change between these two conditions lies the healthy rhythm of the soul's life. Waking and sleeping are really only the extremes of these conditions. When awake the soul is in itself, living its own life; in sleep it loses itself in the universal life of the world, and is therefore to a certain extent freed from itself. The conditions in either direction correspond to the various inner experiences. And the life of thought is a release of the soul from itself, just as feeling, sensation, emotional life, and so forth are the expression of the soul remaining within itself.

Looked at in this way, thought offers to the soul the consolation which it needs when face to face with the feeling of utter loneliness in the world. It is possible to arrive in quite a legitimate way at the feeling, " What am I in the current of universal cosmic events, flowing from one infinity to another —I with my feelings, desires, and will which surely can be of importance to me only! " Directly the life of thought has been rightly realised, this feeling is confronted by another. " The thought which is concerned with these cosmic events draws into itself me and my soul; I am living in those events when I, through thinking, let their being flow into me." It is then possible to feel oneself taken into the universe and secure there. From this condition of the soul, a strength ensues, which the soul feels as though it had come from the cosmic powers themselves, in accordance with wise laws.

It is but another step from this feeling to that in which the soul says, " It is not only I who think, but something thinks in me; the cosmic life expresses itself in me; my soul is only the stage upon which the universe manifests itself as thought."

This feeling may be repudiated by this or that philosophy. It may, with various reasons, be made apparently quite obvious that the thought which has just been expressed, of the world thinking itself in the human soul, is entirely erroneous. In answer to this it must be realised that this thought is one which is worked out through inner experience. Only one who has thus worked it out fully understands its validity, and knows that no refutations can shake that validity. One who has thus mastered it sees from this very thought, quite clearly, what so many ' refutations ' and ' proofs ' are really worth. They may often appear infallible when you still erroneously believe in the convincing power of their content. In that case it is difficult to come to an understanding with people who consider such proofs as conclusive. They are bound to think another person mistaken, because they have not yet accomplished the inner work within themselves which has brought him to a recognition of what seems to them erroneous, or perhaps even absurd.

For one who wishes to find his way into spiritual science, meditations such as the foregoing on thinking are of benefit. For such a person it is a question of bringing his soul into a condition which gives it access to the spiritual world. Access may be denied to the clearest thinking or to the most perfect scientific method, if the soul does not bring anything to meet the spiritual facts, or the information about them ready to press in upon it. It may be a good preparation for the apprehension of spiritual knowledge to have felt frequently what invigorating force there is in the attitude of soul which says, " I feel myself to be one in thought with the stream of cosmic events." In this case it is less a question of the abstract value of this thought as knowledge, than of having often felt in our souls the powerful effect which is experienced when such a thought flows with force through the inner life and circulates like a breath of spiritual life through the soul. It is not only a question of recognising what there is in a thought of this kind, but of experiencing it. The thought is recognised when once it has been present in the soul with sufficient power of conviction; but if it is to ripen and bear fruit which shall promote understanding of the spiritual world, its beings and facts, it must, after having been understood, be made to live in the soul again and again. The soul must again and again be filled with the thought, allowing nothing else to be present in it, and shutting out all other thoughts, feelings, memories, and so forth. Repeated concentration of this kind on such a thoroughly grasped thought draws together forces in the soul which in ordinary life are to some extent dissipated. The soul concentrates and strengthens these forces within itself, and they become the organs for the perception of the spiritual world and its truths.

The right way in which to meditate may be

learned from what has just been pointed out. We first work our way through to a thought which may be realised with the means that lie ready to hand in ordinary life and knowledge. Then we submerge into that thought again and again, and make ourselves completely one with it. The strengthening of the soul is the result of living with a thought which has thus been recognised. In this case the above thought was chosen as an example which was derived from the very nature of thinking. It was chosen as an example because it is very specially fruitful for meditation. But what has been said here holds good, with regard to meditation, for every thought which is acquired in the way that has been described. It is especially fruitful for meditation when we know the state of soul which results from the above-mentioned rhythmic swing in the life of the soul. By that means we arrive in the surest way at the feeling of having been in direct touch with the spiritual world during our meditation.

And this feeling is a sound result of meditation. The force of it should give strength to the rest of our daily life, and not in such a way that an ever-present impression of the meditative state is there the whole time, but so that one feels that from the meditative experience strength is flowing into our whole life.

If the state brought about by meditation extends through daily life as an ever-present impression, it diffuses something which disturbs the mental ease of that life. And the state of meditation itself will not then be sufficiently pure and strong.

14

Meditation gives the best results when through its own character it is kept apart from ordinary life. It influences life in the best way when it is felt to be something distinct from and raised above ordinary life.

II

Concerning Knowledge of the Spiritual World

COMPREHENSION of the facts stated by spiritual science is made easier, if in the ordinary life of the soul attention be given to that which gives rise to ideas capable of such enlargement and transformation that they gradually reach as far as the events and beings of the spiritual world. And unless this path be followed with patience we shall easily be tempted to picture the spiritual world too much like the physical world of the senses. Indeed, unless we follow this path we shall not be able to form a just conception of what is actually spiritual, and of its relation to man.

Spiritual events and beings crowd in upon man when he has prepared his soul to perceive them. The way in which they announce themselves is absolutely different from the way in which physical beings and facts do so. But an idea of this entirely different way of manifesting may be gained if the process of remembering be called to mind. Let us suppose we had an experience some time ago. At a definite moment—from one cause or another—this experience emerges from the depths of psychic life. We know that what so emerges corresponds to an experience, and we relate it to that experience.

16

But at the moment of remembrance there is
of the experience present but only its image in
memory. Now let us imagine an image rising up
in the soul in the same way as does a picture of
memory, yet expressing, not something previously
experienced, but something unfamiliar to the soul.
If we do this, we have formed an idea of the way
in which the spiritual world first makes its appearance
in the soul, when the latter is sufficiently prepared
for it.

Because this is so, one who is not sufficiently con-
versant with the conditions of the spiritual world
will be perpetually bringing forward the objection
that all " presumed " spiritual experiences are
nothing else than more or less indistinct images of
the memory, and that the soul merely does not
recognise them as such and therefore takes them to
be manifestations of a spiritual world. Now it
should on no account be denied that it is difficult
to distinguish between illusions and realities in this
sphere. Many people who believe they have
manifestations from a spiritual world are certainly
only occupied with their own memories, which they
do not recognise as such. In order to see quite
clearly in this respect, it is necessary to be informed
of those numerous sources from which illusion may
arise. We may have seen, for instance, something
only once and for a moment, seen it so hastily that
the impression did not penetrate completely into
the consciousness; and later—perhaps in a quite
different form—it may appear as a vivid picture.
We possibly feel convinced that we never had any-

17

...tter before, and that we have
...tion.

...y other things make it quite
...nat the statements made by those
...persensible sight appear extremely
...to those unacquainted with the special
spiritual science. But one who pays
ca... ...ed to all that is said in my book, *Knowledge of the Higher Worlds and its Attainment*, about the development of spiritual sight, will be put in the way of being able to distinguish between illusion and truth in this sphere.

In this connection, however, the following should also be noted. It is true that spiritual experiences appear in the first place as pictures. It is thus that they rise out of the depths of the soul that is prepared for them. It is then a question of gaining the right relation to these pictures. They only have value for supersensible perception when, by the way in which they present themselves, they show that they are not to be taken for the facts themselves. Directly they are so taken, they are worth little more than ordinary dreams. They must present themselves to us like the letters of an alphabet. We do not look at the shape of the letters, but read in them what is expressed by their means. Just as something written does not call upon us to describe the form of the letters, so the images forming the content of supersensible sight do not call upon us to apprehend them as anything but images; but by their own character they force us to look right through their pictured form and direct our soul's gaze to that

18

which, as a supersensible event or being, is endeavouring to express itself through them.

As little as a person on hearing that a letter contains news previously unknown can deny the possibility of this fact on account of the well-known character of the letters of the alphabet of which it is composed, so little can anybody object to clairvoyant pictures being formed out of well-known objects taken from ordinary life.

It is certainly true, up to a certain point, that the pictures are borrowed from ordinary life, but what is so borrowed is not the important thing to genuine clairvoyant consciousness. The important point is what lies behind and expresses itself through the pictures.

The soul must, of course, first prepare itself for seeing such images appear within its spiritual horizon; but, besides this, it must carefully cultivate the feeling of not stopping short at merely seeing them, but of relating them in the right way to the facts of the supersensible world. It may be said positively that for true clairvoyance there is required not only the capacity for beholding a world of images in oneself, but another faculty as well, which may be compared with reading in the physical world.

The supersensible world is at first to be looked upon as something lying wholly outside man's ordinary consciousness, which has no means of penetrating into that world. The powers of the soul, strengthened by meditation, first bring it into contact with the supersensible world. By means of these the pictures that have been described emerge from the waves of the soul's life. As pictures these are woven entirely by the soul itself. And the materials of which they are made are actually the forces which the soul has acquired for itself in the physical world. The fabric of the pictures is really nothing else but what may be characterised as memory. The clearer we make this to ourselves, in order to understand clairvoyant consciousness, the better. We shall in that case clearly understand that they are but images. And we shall also be cultivating a right understanding of the way in which the images are to be related to the supersensible world. Through the pictures we shall learn to read in the supersensible world. The impressions of the physical world naturally bring us much nearer to the beings and events of that world than the images seen supersensibly bring us to the supersensible world. We might even say that these images are at first like a curtain put up by the soul between it and the supersensible world, when it feels itself to be in contact with that world.

It is a question of becoming gradually familiar with the way in which supersensible things are experienced. Through experience we learn by degrees to read the images, that is, to interpret them correctly. In more important supersensible experiences, their very nature shows that we cannot here have to do with mere pictures of memory from ordinary life. It is indeed true that in this connection many absurd things are asserted by people who have been convinced of certain supersensible facts, or at any rate think they have been. Many people for instance, when convinced of the truth of re-incarnation, at once connect the pictures which arise in their soul with experiences of a former earth-life; but one should always be suspicious when these pictures seem to point to previous earth-lives which are similar in one respect or another to the present one, or which make their appearance in such a way that the present life can, by reasoning, be plausibly explained from the supposed earlier lives. When, in the course of genuine supersensible experience, the true impression of a former earth-life, or of several such lives, appears, it generally happens that the former life or lives are such that we could never have fashioned them or have desired to fashion them in thought by any amount of thinking back from the present life, or out of any wishes and efforts in connection with it. We may, for instance, receive an impression of our former earth existence at some moment during our present life when it is quite impossible to acquire certain faculties, which we had during that former life. So far from its being the case that images appear for the more important spiritual experiences which might be memories of ordinary life, the pictures for these are generally such as we should not have thought of at all in ordinary experience. This tendency increases with real impressions the more purely supersensible the worlds become from which they issue. Thus it is often quite impossible to form images from ordinary life explanatory of the existence between birth and the preceding death. We may find out that in the spiritual life we have developed affection for people and things in complete contrast with the corresponding inclinations we are developing in the present life on earth; and we learn that in our earth-life we have often been driven to be fond of something which in the previous spiritual existence (between death and re-birth) we have rejected and avoided. Any memory of this existence which might be imagined to result from ordinary physical experiences must therefore necessarily be different from the impression we receive through real perception in the spiritual world.

One who is not familiar with spiritual science will certainly make further objections against things being in reality as they have just been described. He will be able to say, for instance: " You are indeed fond of something, but human nature is complicated and secret antipathy is mixed up with every affection. This antipathy to the thing referred to comes up in you at a particular moment. You think it is a prenatal experience, whereas it may perhaps be quite naturally explained from the subsconcious psychic facts of the case." In general there is nothing to be said against such an objection; and in many cases it may be quite correct. Knowledge of clairvoyant consciousness is not easily gained, nor is it without the possibility of objections. But just as it is true that a supposed clairvoyant may be mistaken and regard a subconscious fact as an experience of prenatal spirit-life, so it is also true that a training in spiritual science leads to a knowledge of self which embraces subconscious states of soul and is able to free itself from any illusions with regard to them. Here it need only be asserted that that supersensible knowledge alone is true which at the moment of cognition is able to distinguish what originates from supersensible worlds from that which has merely been shaped by individual imagination. This faculty of discernment becomes so developed by familiarity with supersensible worlds, that perception may in this sphere be as certainly distinguished from imagination, as in the physical world hot iron which is touched with the finger may be distinguished from imaginary hot iron.

III

Concerning Man's Etheric Body and the Elemental World

MAN arrives at the recognition and knowledge of a supersensible spiritual world by overcoming certain obstacles in the way of such a recognition, which at the outset are present in his soul. The difficulty in this case is due to the fact that these obstacles, though affecting the course of the soul's inner experience, are not apprehended as such by ordinary consciousness. For there are many things present, and living, in the human soul, of which at first it knows nothing, and of which it has to gain knowledge by degrees, just as it does of beings and events belonging to the outer world.

The spiritual world, before it is perceived and recognised by the soul, is to the latter something quite strange and unfamiliar, the qualities of which have nothing in common with what the soul is able to learn through its experiences in the physical world. Thus it comes about that the soul may be confronted with the spiritual world and may see in it an absolute void. The soul may feel as though it were looking into an infinite, blank, desolate abyss. Now this feeling actually exists in those depths of the soul of which it is at first unconscious. The feeling is something like fear and dread, and the soul lives in it without being aware of the fact. For the life of the soul is determined not only by what it knows, but by that which is actually present within it, without its knowledge. Now when the soul searches, in the sphere of thought, for reasons for disproving and for evidence against the spiritual world, it does so, not because those reasons are conclusive in themselves, but because it is seeking for a kind of narcotic to dull the feeling just described. People do not deny the existence of the spiritual world, or the possibility of attaining knowledge of it, as a result of being able to prove its non-existence, but because they desire to fill their souls with thoughts which will deceive them and rid them of their dread of the spiritual world. Liberation from this longing for a materialistic narcotic to deaden the dread of the spiritual world cannot be gained till a survey is made of the whole circumstances of this part of the soul's life, as here described. " Materialism as a psychic phenomenon of fear " is an important chapter in the science of the soul.

This dread of the spiritual becomes intelligible when we have won our way through to a recognition of the spiritual; when we have come to see that the events and beings of the physical world are the outward expression of supersensible, spiritual events and beings. We arrive at this understanding when we can see that the body belonging to man, which is perceptible to the senses and with which alone ordinary science is concerned, is the expression of a subtle, supersensible, or etheric body, in which the material or physical body is enclosed, like a denser nucleus, as though in a cloud.

This etheric body is the second principle of human nature. It forms the basis of the life of the physical body. But as regards his etheric body man is not cut off from its corresponding outer world to the same extent to which his physical body is detached from the physical outer world. When we speak of an outer world in connection with the etheric body, it is not the physical outer world, perceived by the senses, that is meant, but a spiritual environment which is as supersensible in relation to the physical world as man's etheric body is in relation to his physical body. Man, as an etheric being, stands in an etheric, or elemental world.

Man is always " experiencing " the fact, although in ordinary life he knows nothing of it, that he, as an etheric being, inhabits an elemental world. When he becomes conscious of this state of things, the consciousness is quite different from that of ordinary experience. This new consciousness sets in when man becomes clairvoyant. The clairvoyant then knows about that which is always present in life, though hidden from ordinary consciousness.

Now in his ordinary consciousness man calls himself " I," signifying the being which presents itself in his physical body. The healthy life of his soul in the world of the senses depends on his thus recognising himself as a being separated from the rest of the world. That healthy psychic life would be interrupted if he characterised any other events or beings of the outer world as part of his ego. When man realises himself as an etheric being in the elemental world, things are different. Then his own ego-being blends with certain occurrences and beings around him. The etheric human being has to find himself in that which is not his inner being, in the same sense as "inner" is conceived in the physical world. In the elemental world there are forces, occurrences, and beings which, although in certain respects part of the outer world, must yet be considered as belonging to one's own ego. As etheric human beings we are woven into the elemental essence of the world. In the physical world we have our thoughts, with which we are so bound up that we may look upon them as forming a constituent part of our ego. But there are forces, occurrences, and so forth which act as intimately upon the inner nature of the etheric human being as thoughts do in the physical world; nor do they behave like thoughts, but are like beings living with and in the soul. Therefore clairvoyance needs a stronger inner force than that which the soul possesses for the purpose of maintaining its own independence in the face of its thoughts. And the essential preparation for true clairvoyance consists in so strengthening and invigorating the soul inwardly, that it can be conscious of itself as an individual being, not only in the presence of its own thoughts, but also when the forces and beings of the elemental world enter the field of its consciousness as if they were a part of its own being.

Now that force of the soul by means of which it maintains its position as a being in the elemental world, is present in man's ordinary life. The soul at first knows nothing of this force, although possessing it. In order to possess it consciously, the soul must first prepare itself. It must acquire that inner force of the soul which is gained during the preparation for clairvoyance. As long as a man cannot make up his mind to acquire this inner force, he has a quite comprehensible dread of recognising his spiritual environment, and he—unconsciously—has recourse to the illusion that the spiritual world does not exist or cannot be known. This illusion delivers him from his instinctive dread of the growing together or blending of his own individual essence, or ego-being, with an actual outer spiritual world.

One who sees into the facts which have been described, comes to recognise an etheric human being behind the physical human being, and a supersensible, etheric, or elemental world behind the one that is physically perceptible.

Clairvoyant consciousness finds in the elemental world real beings which up to a certain point have independence, just as physical consciousness finds thoughts in the physical world which are unreal and have no independence. Growing familiarity with the elemental world leads to seeing these partially independent beings in closer connection with each other. Just as someone may first look upon the limbs of a physical human body as partially independent, and afterwards acknowledge them to be parts

of the body as a whole, so to clairvoyant consciousness are the several beings of the elemental world
embraced within one great spiritual body, of which
they are living members. In the further course of
clairvoyant experience that body comes to be
recognised as the elemental, supersensible, etheric
or life-body of the earth. Within the earth's etheric
body an etheric human being feels himself to be a
member of a whole.

This progress in clairvoyance is a process of
growing familiar with the nature of the elemental
world. That world is inhabited by beings of the
most widely different kinds. If we desire to express
the activity of these force-beings, we can only do
it by portraying their various peculiarities in pictures.
Amongst them are beings which are found to be
allied with everything which makes for endurance,
solidity, and weight. They may be designated as
earth-souls. (And if we do not think ourselves
overwise, and are not afraid of an image which only
points to reality and is not reality itself, we may
speak of them as Gnomes.) We also find beings
which are so constituted that they may be designated
as air, water, and fire souls.

Then again other beings appear. It is true that
they so manifest themselves that they seem to be
elemental or etheric beings, yet it may be seen that
there is something in their etheric nature which is
of higher quality than the essence of the elemental
world. We learn to understand that it is as
impossible to apprehend the real nature of these
beings with the degree of clairvoyance sufficient

only for the elemental world, as it is to arrive at the true nature of man with merely physical consciousness.

The beings mentioned above, which may figuratively be called earth, water, air, and fire souls, are, with the activity proper to them, situated in a certain respect within the earth's elemental etheric body. Their tasks lie there. But the beings of a higher nature which have been characterised carry their activity beyond the earth-sphere. If we come to know them better, through clairvoyant experience, we ourselves and our consciousness are carried in the spirit beyond the sphere of earth. We see how this earth-sphere has been developed from another, and how it is evolving within itself spiritual germs so that in time to come a further sphere, in the sense of a new earth, may arise out of it. My book *Occult Science* explains why that from which the earth was formed may be designated as an " Old Moon-Planet," and why the world towards which the earth aspires in the future may be called Jupiter. The essential point is that by the " Old Moon," we understand a world long gone by, from which the earth has formed itself by transformation; whilst we understand Jupiter, in a spiritual sense, to be a future world, towards which the earth is aspiring.

IV

Summary of the Foregoing

UNDERLYING man's physical being is a subtle, etheric human being which lives in an elemental environment, as physical man lives in a physical environment. The elemental outer world is incorporated in the supersensible life-body of the earth. This latter proves to be the transmuted essence of an earlier or Moon-world, and the preparatory stage of a future world (Jupiter). One may give the foregoing schematically as follows. Man contains:—

I. The physical body, in the surrounding physical material world. Through this body, man comes to recognise himself as an independent, individual being, or ego.

II. The subtle, etheric body in the surrounding elemental world. By its means man comes to recognise himself as a member of the earth's life-body, and hence indirectly as a member of it in three consecutive planetary conditions.

V

Concerning Reincarnation and Karma; Man's Astral Body and the Spiritual World; and Ahrimanic Beings

IT is especially difficult for the soul to recognise that there is something prevailing within its life which is environment to the soul in the same way as the so-called outer world is environment to the ordinary senses. The soul unconsciously resists this, because it imagines its independent existence imperilled by such a fact; and therefore instinctively turns away from it. For though more modern science theoretically admits the existence of the fact, this does not mean that it is as yet fully realised, with all the consequences of inwardly grasping it and becoming permeated with it. If, however, our consciousness can attain to realising it as a vital fact, we learn to discern in the soul's nature an inner nucleus, which exists independently of everything that may be developed in the sphere of the soul's conscious life between birth and death. We learn to know in our own depths a being of which we feel our own self to be the creation, and by which we also feel that our body, the vehicle of consciousness, has been created, with all its powers and attributes.

In the course of this experience the soul learns to feel that a spiritual entity within it is growing to maturity, and that this entity withdraws itself from the influence of conscious life. It begins to feel that this inner entity becomes more and more vigorous, and also more independent, in the course of the life between birth and death. It learns to realise that the entity bears the same relation to the rest of experience, between birth and death, as the developing germ in the being of a plant bears to the sum-total of the plant in which it is developing— with the difference that the germ of the plant is of a physical, whilst the germ of the soul is of a spiritual nature.

The course of such an experience leads one to admit the idea of man's repeated earthly lives. In the nucleus of the soul, which is to a certain degree independent of the soul, the latter is able to feel the germ of a new human life. Into that life the germ will carry over the results of the present one, when it has experienced in a spiritual world after death, in a purely spiritual way, those conditions of life in which it cannot share as long as it is enveloped in a physical earthly body between birth and death.

From this thought there necessarily results another, namely, that the present physical life between birth and death is the product of other lives long past, in which the soul developed a germ which continued to live on in a purely spiritual world after death, till it was ripe for entering upon a new earthly life through a new birth; just as the germ of the plant becomes a new plant when, after having been detached from the old plant in which it was formed, it has been for a while in other conditions of life.

When the soul has been adequately prepared, clairvoyant consciousness learns to immerse itself in the process of the development in one human life of a germ, in a certain way independent, which carries over the results of that life into later earthly lives. In the form of a picture, yet essentially real, as though it were about to reveal itself as an individual entity, there emerges from the waves of the life of the soul a second self, which appears independent of and set over the being which we have previously looked upon as ourself. It seems like an inspirer of that self. And we as this latter self, then flow into one with our inspiring, superior self.

Now our ordinary consciousness lives in this state of things, which is thus beheld by clairvoyant consciousness, without being aware of the fact. Once again it is necessary for the soul to be strengthened, in order that one may hold one's own, not only as regards a spiritual outer world with which one blends, but even as regards a spiritual entity which in a higher sense is one's own self, and which nevertheless stands outside that which is necessarily felt to be the self in the physical world. (The way in which the second self rises out of the waves of the soul's life, in the form of a picture, yet essentially real, is quite different in different human individualities. I have tried in the following plays picturing the soul's life, " The Portal of Initiation," " The Soul's Probation," " The Guardian of the Threshold," and " The Awakening of the Soul," to portray how various human individualities work their way through to the experience of this " other self.")

Now even if the soul in ordinary consciousness knows nothing about its being inspired by its other self, yet that inspirition is nevertheless there, in the depths of the soul. It is, however, not expressed in thoughts or inner words; but takes effect through deeds, through events or through something that happens. It is the other self that guides the soul to the details of its life's destiny, and calls forth capacities, inclinations, aptitudes, and so forth within it. This other self lives in the sum-total or aggregate of the destiny of a human life. It moves alongside of the self which is conditioned by birth and death, and shapes human life, with all that it contains of joy and sorrow. When clairvoyant consciousness joins that other self, it learns to say " I " to the total aggregate of the life-destiny, just as physical man says " I " to his individual being. That which is called by an Eastern word Karma, grows together in the way that has been indicated, with the other self, or the spiritual ego. The life of a human being is seen to be inspired by his own permanent entity, which lives on from one life to another; and the inspiration operates in such a way that the life-destiny of one earthly existence is the direct consequence of previous ones.

Thus man learns to know himself as another being, different from his physical personality, which indeed only comes to expression in physical existence through the working of this being. When the consciousness enters the world of that other being, it is in a region which, as compared with the elemental world, may be called the world of the spirit.

As long as we feel ourselves to be in that world, we find ourselves completely outside the sphere in which all the experiences and events of the physical world are enacted. We look from another world back upon the one which we have in a certain sense left behind. But we also arrive at the knowledge that, as human beings, we belong to both worlds. We feel the physical world to be a kind of reflected image of the world of the spirit. Yet this image, although reflecting the events and beings of the spiritual world, does not merely do this, but also leads an independent life of its own, although it is only an image. It is as though a person were to look into a mirror, and as though his reflected image were to come to independent life whilst he was looking at it.

Moreover, we learn to know spiritual beings who bring about this independent life of the reflected image of the spiritual world. We feel them to be beings who belong to the world of the spirit with regard to their origin, but who have left the arena of that world, and sought their field of action in the physical world. We thus find ourselves confronting two worlds which act one upon the other.

We will call the spiritual world the higher, and the physical world the lower.

We learn to know these spiritual beings in the lower world through having to a certain extent transferred our point of view to the higher world. One class of these spiritual beings presents itself in such a way that through them we discover the reason why man experiences the physical world as substantial and material. We discover that everything material is in reality spiritual, and that the spiritual activity of these beings consolidates and hardens the spiritual element of the physical world into matter. However unpopular certain names are in the present day, they are needed for that which is seen as reality in the world of spirit. And so we will call the beings who bring about materialisation the Ahrimanic beings. It appears that their original sphere is the mineral kingdom. In that kingdom they reign in such a way that there they can bring fully into manifestation what is their real nature. In the vegetable kingdom and in the higher kingdoms of nature they accomplish something else, which only becomes intelligible when the sphere of the elemental world is taken into account. Seen from the world of the spirit, the elemental world also appears like a reflection of that world. But the reflected image in the elemental world has not so much independence as that in the physical world. In the former, the spiritual beings of the Ahrimanic class are less dominant than in the latter. From the elemental world, however, they do develop amongst other things, the kind of activity which comes to expression in annihilation and death. We may even say that in the higher kingdoms of nature the part of the Ahrimanic beings is to introduce death. So far as death is part of the necessary order of existence, the mission of the Ahrimanic beings is legitimate.

But when we view the activity of the Ahrimanic beings from the world of the spirit, we find that something else is connected with their work in the lower world. Inasmuch as their sphere of action is there, they do not feel bound to respect the limits which would restrain their activity if they were operating in the higher world from which they originate. In the lower world they struggle for an independence which they could never have in the higher sphere. This is especially evident in the influence of the Ahrimanic beings on man, inasmuch as man forms the highest kingdom of nature in the physical world. As far as the human life of the soul is bound up with physical existence, they strive to give that life independence, to wrench it free from the higher world, and to incorporate it entirely in their own world. Man as a thinking soul originates from the higher world. The thinking soul which has become clairvoyant also enters that higher world. But the thinking which is evolved in, and bound up with, the physical world, has in it that which must be called the influence of the Ahrimanic beings. These beings desire to give, as it were, a kind of permanent existence to a sense-bound thinking within the physical world. At the same time as their forces bring death, they desire to hold back the thinking soul from death, and only to allow the other principles of man to be carried away by the stream of annihilation. Their intention is that the human power of thought shall remain behind in the physical world and adopt a kind of existence approximating more and more to the Ahrimanic nature.

In the lower world what has just been described is only expressed through its effects. Man may strive to saturate himself in his thinking soul with the forces which recognise the spiritual world, and know themselves to live and have their being within it. But he may also turn away with his thinking soul from those forces, and only make use of his thought for laying hold of the physical world. Temptations to the latter course of action come from the Ahrimanic powers.

VI

Concerning the Astral Body and the Luciferic Beings; and the Nature of the Etheric Body

THERE is another group of spiritual beings, who from the world of the spirit are seen to be active in the physical world (and also in the elemental world), as in an adopted field of action. These are the spirits who desire to liberate the feeling soul entirely from the physical world, and therefore in a certain way to spiritualise it. Life in the physical world is part of the cosmic order of things. While the human soul is living in the physical world, it is passing through a development which is part of the conditions of its existence. Its being woven into the physical world is a result of the activity of beings whom one learns to know in the higher world. That activity is opposed by the beings who desire to wrench the feeling soul free from physical conditions. These latter beings may be called the Luciferic beings.

The Luciferic beings stand in the physical world searching as it were, for everything of a psychic nature (feeling) which is to be found there, in order that they may draw it out of the physical world and incorporate it in a cosmic sphere of their own, adapted to their nature. Seen from the higher world, the activity of these Luciferic beings is also observable in the elemental world. Within this they strive to obtain a certain sphere of power which they want to disconnect from the grossness of the physical world, although that sphere has been pre-ordained, by the beings of the higher world, to be connected with this sense-world. Just as the Ahrimanic beings would be keeping to their own sphere if they were only to bring about the temporary annihilation of existence which is based on the order of the cosmos, so the Luciferic beings would not be crossing the boundary of their own kingdom if they imbued the feeling soul with powers which would continually stimulate it to rise above the urgent necessities of the physical world, and feel itself, with regard to those necessities, a free and independent being. But the Luciferic beings go beyond the limits of their domain when they desire, in the face of the universal order of the higher world, to create a special spiritual kingdom for which they wish to remould the psychic beings in the physical world.

We can see how the influence of Luciferic beings in the physical world expands in two directions. On the one hand it is owing to them that man is able to rise above the bare experience of what is physically real. He is able to derive his joy, his uplifting, not only from the physical world; but can also take pleasure in and feel elated by that which exists merely in semblance, that which as beauty transcends the physical. From this point of view the Luciferic beings have co-operated in bringing about the most important, and especially the artistic, features of civilisation. Moreover, man is able to enjoy unfettered thought; he need not merely describe physical things and portray them slavishly in his thoughts. He is able to develop creative thought beyond the physical world, and to philosophise about things. On the other hand, the exaggeration of the Luciferic forces in the soul is the source of much extravagance and confusion, for they try to develop the activities of the soul without adhering to the conditions of the higher cosmic order. Philosophising which is not based upon a thorough adherence to the cosmic order, headstrong indulgence in arbitrary ideas, excessive forcing of one's own personal predilections: all these things are the dark side of the Luciferic activity.

The human soul belongs, through its other self, to the higher world. But it also belongs to existence in the lower world. Clairvoyant consciousness, if it has passed through adequate preparation, feels itself as a conscious being in the higher world. The facts of the case are not altered, but, to those facts which hold good for every human soul, there is added in clairvoyant consciousness, the knowledge of the facts. Every human soul belongs to the higher world, and when man is living in the physical world, he is associated with a physical body which is subject to the processes of the physical world. The soul is also associated with a subtle, etheric body, which lives subject to the processes of the elemental world. The Ahrimanic and Luciferic forces, which are spiritual and supersensible, work in both these bodies.

In so far as the human soul lives in the higher or spiritual world, it is what may be called an astral being. One of the many reasons which justify this expression is that the astral being of man as such is not subject to the conditions which prevail within the sphere of earth. Spiritual science recognises that within man's astral being are working, not the terrestrial ' laws of nature,' but those laws which have to be taken into account in considering the processes of the world of the stars (astra). On this account the term may appear justified. Thus the recognition of a third or astral body is added to that of the physical body and the subtle, etheric body of man. But it is necessary that the following should be borne in mind. As regards its original essence, man's astral body has its origin in the higher world, in the spiritual world proper. Within that sphere it is a being of the same nature as other beings whose activity is exercised in that world. Inasmuch then as the elemental and physical worlds are reflections of the spiritual world, the etheric and physical bodies of man must also be looked upon as reflections of his astral being. But in those bodies forces are working which originate ·from the Luciferic and Ahrimanic beings. Now since those beings have a spiritual origin, it is natural that within the region of the etheric and physical bodies themselves there should be found a kind of human astral essence. And a degree of clairvoyance which merely accepts the pictures of clairvoyant consciousness, without being able rightly to understand their meaning, may easily take the astral admixture in the physical and etheric bodies for the astral body proper. Yet that human astral essence is just that principle of human nature which opposes man's conforming to the laws really suitable for him in the order of the cosmos. Mistakes and confusions are more easily made in this domain because a knowledge of the soul's astral being is at the outset quite impossible for ordinary human consciousness. Even during the first stages of clairvoyant consciousness such knowledge is not yet attainable. This consciousness is attained when man experiences himself in his etheric body. But in this body he beholds the reflected images of his other self, and the higher world to which he belongs. In this way also he beholds the reflected etheric image of his astral body, and at the same time the Luciferic and Ahrimanic beings which that body contains.

It will be shewn later in this work that the ego too, which man in ordinary life looks upon as his entity, is not the real ego, but only the reflection of the real ego in the physical sense-world. In the same way the etheric reflection of the astral body may, in etheric clairvoyance, become an illusory image mistaken for the real astral body.

When one penetrates further into the higher world, clairvoyant consciousness also succeeds in gaining a true insight as regards the human being into the nature of the reflection of the higher world in the lower. It then becomes supremely evident that the subtle, etheric body, which man bears about him in his present earthly existence, is not really the reflected image of that which corresponds to this body in the higher world. It is a reflected image altered by the activity of the Luciferic and Ahrimanic beings. The spiritual archetype of the etheric body is not able to reflect itself at all perfectly in man on earth, owing to the nature of the earthly essence in which the beings mentioned above are active. If clairvoyant consciousness betakes itself beyond the earth to a region in which a perfect reflection of the archetype of the etheric body is possible, it finds itself carried back to a remote past, previous to the present condition of the earth, before even the " Moon condition " which preceded it. It arrives at an insight into the manner in which the present earth has evolved out of a " Moon condition," and the latter again out of a " Sun condition." Further particulars as to why the terms " Sun " and " Moon " condition are justified will be found in my *Occult Science.*

The earth, then, was once in a Sun condition, out of which it evolved to a Moon condition, and afterwards became Earth. During the Sun condition the etheric body of man was an absolute reflection of the spiritual events and beings of the world from which it originates. Clairvoyant consciousness discovers that those Sun beings consisted of pure wisdom. Thus we may say that, during the earth's Sun condition in a remote past, man received his etheric body as a pure reflection of cosmic beings of Wisdom. Later, during the Moon and Earth conditions, the etheric body has become changed into that which it is now as a part of the human being.

VII

Summary of the Foregoing

MAN bears within him a soul-centre belonging to a spiritual world. This is the permanent human entity, which passes through repeated earthly lives in such a way that in one earthly life it is trained in normal consciousness as a being independent of that consciousness, then experiences itself in a purely spiritual world, after human physical death, and in due time realises in a new earthly life the results of the preceding one. This permanent entity acts as the inspirer of man's destiny in such a way that one earthly life follows others as a consequence which is based on the order of the cosmos.

Man is this permanent entity itself; he lives in it as though in his other self. Inasmuch as he, as a being, is that other self, so he lives in an astral body, in the same way as he is living in a physical and etheric body. Just as the environment of the physical body is the physical world and that of the etheric body the elemental world, so the environment of the astral body is the world of the spirit.

Beings of the same nature and origin as man's other self are working in the physical and elemental worlds as Ahrimanic and Luciferic powers. The way in which they work makes the relation of the astral body to the etheric and physical bodies intelligible.

46

The original source of the etheric body is to be found in a long-past period of the earth, its so-called Sun condition.

In accordance with the foregoing, the following survey of man may be made:—

I.   The physical body in the environment of the physical world. By means of this body man recognises himself as an independent individual (ego).

II.   The subtle (etheric) life-body in the elemental environment.   By means of this body man recognises himself as a member of the earth's life-body, and hence indirectly as a member of three successive planetary states.

III.   The astral body in a purely spiritual environment.   Through this body man is a member of a spiritual world of which the elemental and physical worlds are reflections.   In the astral body lives man's other self, and this comes to expression in repeated earthly lives.

VIII

Concerning the Guardian of the Threshold and some Peculiarities of Clairvoyant Consciousness

AS far as his experiences in the physical world are concerned, man is outside the spiritual world, in which, as has been stated in the preceding pages, his real being is rooted. The part played by physical experience in human nature is realised when we consider that for clairvoyant consciousness, which enters the supersensible worlds, it is necessary to strengthen those very forces of the soul which are acquired in the physical world. If this strengthening has not taken place, the soul feels a certain timidity in entering the supersensible world. It even tries to avoid an entrance by seeking proofs of its impossibility.

But if the soul finds that it is strong enough to enter, if it recognises in itself the forces which allow it, after entering, to maintain itself there as an independent being, and to experience in its field of consciousness not only thoughts but beings, as must be the case in the elemental and spiritual worlds, then the soul also feels that only by life in the physical world has it been enabled to gather those forces. It realises the necessity of being led through the physical world on its journey through the universe.

The realisation of this especially results from the experience with regard to *thinking* through which clairvoyant consciousness passes. On entering the elemental world, the consciousness becomes filled with beings who are perceived in the form of pictures. In that world it is not able to develop with regard to these beings an inner activity of the soul similar to that which is developed in thought-life within the physical world. Yet it would be impossible to find one's way as a human being within the elemental world if we did not enter it as thinking beings. We might certainly behold the beings of the elemental world without thinking about them, but we should not know what any of them really were. We should be like a man looking at writing which he cannot read; he sees with his eyes exactly the same thing as is seen by one who can read it, but it only has meaning and substance for the latter.

Nevertheless clairvoyant consciousness during its sojourn in the elemental world exercises by no means the same kind of thought-activity as is carried on in the physical world. Rather is it the case that a thinking being—such as man—in the act of beholding the elemental world also perceives the meaning of its beings and forces, while a non-thinking being would see the pictures without understanding their meaning and essence.

On entering the spiritual world, the Ahrimanic beings, for instance, would be taken for something quite different from what they really are if they were not beheld by the soul as a thinking being. It is the same with the Luciferic and other beings of the spiritual world. The Ahrimanic and Luciferic beings are only beheld by man in their true reality if he contemplates them from the spiritual world with clairvoyant sight which has been strengthened by thinking.

If the soul did not arm itself with adequate power for thought, the Luciferic beings, when seen from the spiritual world, would take possession of the world of clairvoyant pictures and bring about in the contemplating soul the illusion that it was penetrating ever more deeply into the spiritual world which it was really seeking, whereas actually it would be sinking deeper and deeper into the world which the Luciferic forces desire to prepare similar to their own being. The soul would certainly feel itself becoming more independent, but it would be adapting itself to a spiritual world not in keeping with its own nature and origin. It would be entering a spiritual environment foreign to it.

The physical world conceals from view such beings as the Luciferic ones. Therefore, within that world they are not able to mislead the consciousness. They are simply non-existent as far as this consciousness is concerned, and, not being misled by them, it is able to strengthen itself adequately by thought. It is one of the instinctive peculiarities of healthy consciousness that it only desires to enter the spiritual world in proportion as it has sufficiently strengthened itself in the physical world for beholding the spiritual world. Consciousness clings to the way in which it can experience itself in the physical world. It feels itself to be in its own element when it can experience itself by means of the thoughts, feelings, emotions, etc., which it owes to the physical world. The tenacity with which consciousness clings to this kind of experience is especially apparent at the actual moment of entering supersensible worlds. Just as a person at particular moments of his life clings to dear memories, so at the entrance to supersensible worlds do there of necessity ascend from the depths of the soul all possible affections of which the individual is capable. We then become aware how strongly we cleave to that life which connects man with the physical world. This attachment to earth-life then appears in its full reality, stripped of our usual illusions. At the entrance to the supersensible world, and, as it were, at the first supersensible achievement—a certain self-knowledge is brought about, of which we can previously have had scarcely any idea. And we see how much we have to leave behind if we really desire to enter knowingly into that world in which, after all, we are always actually present. What we have made of ourselves as human beings, consciously and unconsciously, in the physical world comes before the soul with the most vivid distinctness.

The result of this experience is often that all further attempts at penetrating into supersensible worlds are abandoned. For we then clearly realise the necessity of changing our way of thinking and feeling, if our sojourn in the spiritual world is to be successful. We have to make up our minds to develop quite a different attitude of soul from the one that has hitherto been ours, or, in other words, a different attitude must be added to the one we have already acquired.

And yet—what is it that really happens at the moment of entering the supersensible world? We see the being which we have always been; but we do not now see it from the physical word, from which we have always seen it hitherto; we see it, free from illusions, in its true reality, from the standpoint of the spiritual world. We behold it in such a way that we feel ourselves permeated with those powers of cognition which are able to measure it according to its spiritual worth. When we see ourselves thus, it becomes plain why we hesitate about consciously entering the supersensible world; the degree of strength becomes apparent, which it is necessary to have before entering it. We see how, even with knowledge, we keep at a distance from that world. And the more accurately we thus see through ourselves, the more strongly do those affections come to the front by means of which we desire to continue to keep our consciousness in the physical world. Our increased knowledge entices those affections out of their lurking-places in the depths of the soul. We must, however, recognise them, for only by so doing are they overcome. But even when recognised they still manifest their power in quite a remarkable way. They desire to subdue the soul, which feels itself drawn down by them as if into unknown depths. The moment of self-recognition is a serious one. Far too much philosophising and theorising about self-knowledge goes on in the world. The soul's gaze is thereby rather turned away from, than drawn towards, the earnestness connected with real self-knowledge. And yet, in spite of this necessary earnestness, it affords a great satisfaction to know that human nature is so ordered that its instincts prevent it from entering the spiritual world before it is able to develop within itself, as self-experience, the necessary state of maturity. What a satisfaction it is that the first momentous meeting with a being of the supersensible world is the meeting with our own being in its true reality which will guide us further in human evolution.

We may say that there is hidden within man a being that keeps careful watch and ward on the boundary which has to be crossed at the entrance to the supersensible world. This spiritual being, hidden in man, which is man himself, but which he can as little perceive with ordinary consciousness as the eye can see itself, is the 'Guardian of the Threshold' of the spiritual world. We learn to recognise him at the moment at which we are not only actually he, but also confronting him, as though we were standing outside him, and he were another being.

As with other experiences of supersensible worlds, it is the strengthened and reinforced faculties of the soul which make visible the Guardian of the Threshold. For, setting aside the fact that the meeting with the Guardian becomes raised into knowledge by clairvoyant spiritual sight, that meeting is not an event which happens only to the man who has become clairvoyant. Exactly the same fact as is represented by this meeting happens to every human being every time he falls asleep, and we are confronting ourselves—which is the same thing as standing before the Guardian of the Threshold—for as long as our sleep lasts. During sleep the soul rises to its supersensible nature. But its inner forces are not then strong enough to bring about consciousness of itself.

In order to understand clairvoyant experience, especially in its early beginnings, it is particularly important to bear in mind that the soul may already have begun to live in the supersensible world before it is able to formulate to itself any knowledge worthy of the name. Clairvoyance at first appears in a very delicate way, so that often, inasmuch, as they expect to see something almost tangible, people do not heed clairvoyant impressions which are flitting by, and will in no way recognise them as such. In this case the impressions sink into oblivion almost as soon as they appear. They enter the field of consciousness so slightly that they remain quite unnoticed, like tiny clouds on the soul's horizon.

On this account, and because people for the most part expect clairvoyance to be quite different from what it at first is, it often remains undiscovered by many earnest seekers after the spiritual world. In this respect too the meeting with the Guardian of the Threshold is important. If the soul has been strengthened just in the direction of self-knowledge, this very meeting may merely be like the first gentle flitting-by of a spiritual vision; but it will not be so easily consigned to oblivion as other supersensible impressions, because people are more interested in their own being than in other things.

There is, however, no need at all that the meeting with the Guardian should be one of the first clairvoyant experiences. The soul may be strengthened in various directions, and the first of such directions may bring other beings or events within its spiritual horizon before the meeting with the Guardian takes place. Yet this meeting is sure to occur comparatively soon after entering the supersensible world.

IX

Concerning the Ego-Feeling and the Human Soul's Capacity for Love; and the Relation of these to the Elemental World

WHEN the human soul consciously enters the elemental world, it finds itself obliged to change many of the ideas which it acquired in the physical world; but if the soul strengthens its forces to a corresponding degree, it will be quite fit for the change. Only if it shrinks from the effort of this acquiring strength, may it be seized by the feeling of losing, on entering the elemental world, the firm basis on which it must build up its inner life. The ideas which are gained in the physical world only offer an impediment to entering the elemental world as long as we try to keep them in exactly the same form in which we gained them. There is, however, no reason except habit for adhering to them in this way. It is also quite natural that the consciousness, which at first only lives in the physical world, should be accustomed to look upon the form of its ideas which it has shaped there, as the only possible one. And it is even more than natural, it is necessary. The life of the soul would never attain its inner solidarity, its necessary stability, if it did not develop a consciousness in the physical world which in a certain respect lived in fixed ideas, rigorously forced upon it. Through everything which life in the physical world can give the soul, is it able to enter the elemental world in such a way that it does not lose its independence and firmness of nature there. Strengthening and reinforcement of the life of the soul must be gained in order that that independence may not only be present as an unconscious quality of the soul on entering the elemental world, but may also be kept clearly in the consciousness. If the soul is too weak for conscious experience in the elemental world, on entering it the independence vanishes just as a thought does which is not imprinted with sufficient clearness on the soul to live on as a distinct memory. In this case the soul cannot really enter the supersensible world at all with its consciousness. When it makes the attempt to enter, it is again and again thrown back into the physical world, by the being living within the soul which may be called the Guardian of the Threshold. And even if the soul has, so to speak, nibbled at the supersensible world, so that on sinking back into the physical world it retains something of the supersensible in its consciousness, such spoil from another sphere often only causes confusion in the life of thought. It is quite impossible to fall into such confusion if the faculty of sound judgment, as it may be acquired in the physical world, be adequately cultivated. By thus reinforcing the faculty of judgment, the soul will develop the right relation to the events and beings of supersensible worlds. For in order to live consciously in those worlds, an attitude of the soul is necessary which cannot be developed in the physical world with the same intensity with which it appears in supersensible worlds. This is the attitude of surrender to what is being experienced. We must steep ourselves in the experience and identify ourselves with it; and we must be able to do this to such a degree that we see ourselves outside our own being and feel ourselves within some other being. A transformation of our own being into the other with which we are having the experience must take place. If we do not possess this faculty of transformation, we cannot experience anything genuine in supersensible worlds. For there all experience is due to our being able to realise this feeling, " Now I am transformed in a certain definite way; now I am vitally present in a being which through its nature transforms mine in this particular way." This transformation of self, this conscious projection of oneself into other beings, is life in supersensible worlds. By this process of conscious self-projection into others, we learn to know the beings and events of those worlds. We come to notice that with one being we have a certain degree of affinity; but that, by virtue of our own nature, we are further removed from another. Variations of inner experience come into view which, especially in the elemental world, we must call sympathies and antipathies. For on encountering a being or event of the elemental world, we feel an experience emerging in the soul which may be denoted sympathy. By this experience we recognise the nature of the elemental being or event. But we must not think that experiences of sympathy and antipathy are only of account in proportion to their intensity or degree. In the physical world it is indeed in a certain sense true that we only speak of a strong or weak sympathy or antipathy as the case may be. In the elemental world, sympathies and antipathies are not only distinguishable by their intensity, but also in the same way as, for instance, colours may be distinguished from each other in the physical world. Just as we have a physical world of many colours, so can we experience an elemental world containing many sympathies or antipathies. It has also to be taken into account that antipathy in the elemental realm does not carry with it the meaning that we inwardly turn away from the thing so described; by antipathetic we simply mean a quality of the elemental being or event which bears a similar relation to the sympathetic quality of another event or being as does blue to red in the physical world.

We may speak of a " sense " which man is able to awaken for the elemental world in his etheric body. This sense is capable of perceiving sympathies and antipathies in the elemental world just as the eye becomes aware of colours and the ear of sounds in the physical world. And just as there one object is red and another blue, so the beings of the elemental world are such that one radiates a certain kind of sympathy, and another a certain kind of antipathy to our spiritual sight.

This experience of the elemental world through sympathies and antipathies is again something not confined to the clairvoyantly awakened soul; it

is always at hand for every human soul, being part
of its nature. But in the ordinary life of the soul
the knowledge of this part of human nature is not
developed. Man bears within him his etheric body;
and through it is connected in manifold ways with
beings and events of the elemental world. At one
moment of his life he is woven with sympathies and
antipathies into the elemental world in one way; at
another moment in another way.

The soul, however, cannot continuously so live
as an etheric being that sympathies and antipathies
are always active and clearly expressed within it.
Just as waking life alternates with sleep in physical
existence, so does a different state contrast with that
of experiencing sympathies and antipathies in the
elemental world. The soul may withdraw from all
sympathies and antipathies and experience itself
alone, regarding and feeling merely its own being.
Indeed, this feeling may reach such a degree of
intensity that we may speak of *willing* our own
being. It is then a question of a condition of the
soul's life not easy to describe, because in its pure,
original nature it is of such a kind that nothing in
the physical world resembles it except the strong,
unalloyed ego-feeling or feeling of self in the soul.
As far as the elemental world is concerned we may
describe this state as one in which the soul feels the
impulse to say to itself with regard to the necessary
surrender to experiences of sympathy and antipathy: " I will keep entirely to myself and within
myself." And through a kind of unfolding of the
will the soul wrenches itself free from the state of

surrender to the elemental experiences of sympathy and antipathy. This life in the self is, as it were, the sleeping state of the elemental world; whereas the surrender to events and beings is the waking state. When the human soul is awake in the elemental world and develops a wish to experience itself only, that is to say, feels the need of elemental sleep, it can obtain this by returning to the waking state of physical life with a fully developed feeling of self. For such experience, saturated with the feeling of self, in the physical world is synonymous with elemental sleep. It consists in the soul's being torn away from elemental experiences. It is literally true that to clairvoyant consciousness the life of the soul in the physical world is a spiritual sleep.

When awakening to the supersensible world takes place in rightly developed human clairvoyance, the memory of the soul's experiences in the physical world still remains. It must remain, otherwise other beings and events would be present in clairvoyant consciousness, but not the clairvoyant's own being. We should in that case have no knowledge of ourselves; we should not be living in the spirit ourselves; but other beings and events would be living in our soul. Taking this into consideration, it will be clear that rightly developed clairvoyance must lay great streess on the cultivation of a strong ego-feeling. This ego-feeling developed with clairvoyance is by no means something which only enters the soul through clairvoyance; it is merely that we get to know that which always exists in the depths of the soul, but which remains unknown to the soul's ordinary life as it runs its course in the physical world.

The strong ego-feeling is not there through the etheric body as such, but through the soul which experiences itself in the physical body. If the soul does not bring that feeling with it into the clairvoyant state from its experience in the physical world, it will prove insufficiently equipped for experience in the elemental world.

On the other hand, it is essential for human consciousness within the physical world that the soul's feeling of self, its experience of the ego, although it must exist, should be modified. By this means it is possible for the soul to undergo within the physical world training for the noblest of moral forces, that of fellow-feeling, or feeling with another. If the strong ego-feeling were to project itself into the soul's conscious experiences within the physical world, moral impulses and ideas could not develop in the right way. They could not bring forth the fruit of love. But the faculty of self-surrender, a natural impulse in the elemental world, is not to be put on a par with what is called love in human experience. Elemental self-surrender means experiencing oneself in another being or event; love is the experiencing another being in one's own soul. In order to develop the latter experience, the feeling of self, or ego-experience, present in the depths of the soul, must have, as it were, a veil drawn over it; and in consequence of the soul's own forces being thus dulled, one is able to feel within oneself the sorrows and joys of the other being: love, which is the source of all genuine morality in human life, springs up. Love is the most important result for man of his experience in the physical world. If we analyse the nature of love or fellow-feeling, we find it is the way in which spiritual reality is expressed in the physical world. It has already been said that it is in the nature of what is supersensible to become transformed into something else. If what is spiritual in man as he lives the physical life becomes so transformed that it dulls the ego-feeling and lives again as love, the spiritual remains true to its own elemental laws. We may say that on becoming clairvoyantly conscious the human soul awakes in the spiritual world; but we must say just as much that in love the spiritual awakens in the physical world. Where love and fellow-feeling are stirring in life, we sense the magic breath of the spirit, interpenetrating the physical world. Hence rightly developed clairvoyance can never weaken sympathy or love. The more completely the soul becomes at home in spiritual worlds, the more it feels loveless-ness and lack of fellow-feeling to be a denial of spirit itself.

The experiences of consciousness which is becom-ing clairvoyant, manifest special peculiarities with regard to what has just been stated. Whereas the ego-feeling—necessary as it is for experience in supersensible worlds—is easily deadened, and often behaves like a weak, fading thought in the memory, feelings of hatred and lovelessness, and immoral impulses become intense experiences immediately after entering the supersensible world. They appear before the soul like reproaches come to life, and become terribly real pictures. In order not to be tormented by them, clairvoyant consciousness often has recourse to the expedient of looking about for spiritual forces which weaken the impressions of these pictures. But by doing so the soul steeps itself in these forces, which have an injurious effect on the newly-won clairvoyance. They drive it out of the good regions of the spiritual world, and towards the bad ones.

On the other hand, true love and real kindness of heart are experiences of the soul which strengthen the forces of consciousness in the way necessary for acquiring clairvoyance. When it is said that the soul needs preparation before it is able to have experiences in the supersensible world, it should be added that one of the many means of preparation is the capacity for true love, and the disposition towards genuine human kindness and fellow-feeling.

An over-developed ego-feeling in the physical world works against morality. An ego-feeling too feebly developed causes the soul, around which the storms of elemental sympathies and antipathies are actually playing to be lacking in inner firmness and stability. These qualities can only exist when a sufficiently strong ego-feeling is working out of the experiences of the physical world upon the etheric body, which of course remains unknown in ordinary life. But in order to develop a really moral temper of mind it is necessary that the ego-feeling, though it must exist, should be moderated by feelings of good-fellowship, sympathy, and love.

X

Concerning the Boundary between the Physical World and Supersensible Worlds

IN order to understand the mutual relations of the various worlds, we must take into account the fact that a force which in one world is bound to develop activity in conformity with the order of the universe, may, when it comes to be developed in another world, be directed against that order. Therefore it is necessary for man's being that there should exist in his etheric body the two opposing forces, the capacity for transformation into other beings, and the strong ego-feeling, or feeling of self. Neither of these forces of the human soul can be unfolded in physical existence except in a deadened form. In the elemental world they exist in such a way as to make man's being possible by their mutual balance, just as sleep and the waking state make human life in the physical world possible. The relation of two such opposing forces can never be that of one effacing the other, but must be of such a kind that both are developed and act upon each other in the way of balance or compensation.

Now it is only in the elemental world that the ego-feeling and the capacity for transformation act upon each other in the way indicated; the physical world can only be worked upon, in conformity with the order of the universe, by the result of these two forces in their mutual relationship and co-operation. If the capacity for transformation which it is necessary for a person to possess in his etheric body were to extend in the same degree to physical existence, he would feel himself in his soul as something which in considering his physical body he is not. The physical body gives man in its own world a certain fixed stamp, by means of which he is put into that world as a particular personal being. He is not put into the elemental world with his etheric body in this manner. In the elemental world, in order to be a human being in the full sense, he must be able to assume the most varied forms. If this were impossible to him, he would be condemned to complete isolation in the elemental world; he would not be able to know about anything in it except himself; for he would not feel himself related to any other being or event. But this, in the elemental world would be equivalent to the non-existence of those beings or events, as far as such a person was concerned.

If, however, the human soul were to develop in the physical world the capacity for transformation necessary for the elemental world, its personal identity would be lost. Such a soul would be living in contradiction with itself. In the physical world, the capacity for transformation must be a power at rest in the depths of the soul; a power which gives the soul its fundamental tone or keynote, but which does not come to development in that world.

Clairvoyant consciousness has therefore to live itself into the capacity for transformation; if it were not able to do this, it could make no observations in the elemental world. It thus acquires a faculty which it should only bring to bear as long as it knows itself to be in the elemental world, and which it must suppress as soon as it returns to the physical world. Clairvoyant consciousness must ever observe the boundary of the two worlds, and must not use in the physical world faculties adapted for a supersensible world. If the soul, knowing itself to be in the physical world, were to allow the capacity for transformation possessed by its etheric body to go on working, ordinary consciousness would become filled with conceptions which do not correspond to any being in the physical world. Confusion would reign in the life of the soul's thought. Observation of the boundary between the worlds is a necessary presupposition for the right working of clairvoyant consciousness. One who wants to acquire this consciousness must be careful that no disturbing element creeps into his ordinary consciousness through his knowledge of supersensible worlds.

If we learn to know the Guardian of the Threshold we know the state of our soul with regard to the physical world, and whether it is strong enough to banish from physical consciousness the forces and faculties, belonging to supersensible worlds, which should not be allowed to be active in ordinary consciousness. If the supersensible world is entered without the self-knowledge brought about by the

Guardian of the Threshold, we may be over-whelmed by the experiences of that world. These experiences may thrust themselves into physical consciousness as illusive pictures. In that case they assume the character of sense-perceptions, and the necessary consequence is that the soul takes them for realities when they are not so. Rightly developed clairvoyance will never take the pictures of the elemental world for reality in the sense in which physical consciousness has to take the experiences of the physical world as realities. The pictures of the elemental world are only brought into their true association with the realities to which they correspond, by the soul's faculty of transformation.

Again, the second force necessary for the etheric body—the strong ego-feeling—should not be pro-jected into the soul's life within the physical world in the same way as is appropriate for it in the elemental world. If it is, it then becomes a source of immoral propensities, as far as these are con-nected with egoism. It is at this point in its observa-tion of the universe that spiritual science finds the origin of evil in human action. It would be mis-understanding the order of the world to surrender oneself to the belief that this order could be main-tained without the forces which form the source of evil. If these forces were non-existent, the etheric being of man could not come to development in the elemental world. These forces are entirely good when they come into operation in the elemental world only. They bring about evil when they do not remain at rest in the depths of the soul, there regulating man's relation to the elemental world, but are transferred to the soul's experience within the physical world and are changed thereby into selfish impulses. In this case they work against the faculty of love and thus become the causes of immoral action.

If the strong ego-feeling passes from the etheric to the physical body, it not only effects a strengthening of egoism, but a weakening of the etheric body. Clairvoyant consciousness has to make the discovery that on entering the supersensible world, the necessary ego-feeling is weak in proportion as egoism in the experiences of the physical world is strong. Egoism does not make a human being strong in the depths of his soul, but weak. And when man passes through the gateway of death, the effect of the egoism which has been developed during the life between birth and death is such as to make the soul weak for the experiences of the supersensible world.

XI

Concerning Beings of the Spirit-Worlds

IF the soul enters the supersensible world with
clairvoyant consciousness, it learns to know itself
there in a way of which in the physical world it can
have no conception. It finds that through its
faculty of transformation it becomes acquainted
with beings to whom it is more or less related; but
in addition to this it becomes aware of meeting
beings in the supersensible world to whom it is not
only related, but with whom it must compare
itself, in order to know itself. And it further
observes that these beings in supersensible worlds
have become what the soul itself, through its
adventures and experiences in the physical world,
has become. In the elemental world beings con-
front the human soul who have developed within
that world powers and faculties which man himself
can only unfold through still having about him his
physical body, in addition to his etheric body and
the other supersensible principles of his being.
The beings here alluded to have no such body with
physical senses. They have so evolved that through
their etheric body they have a soul-nature such as
man has through his physical body. Although to
a certain degree they are beings of like nature to
himself, they differ from him in not being subject

to the conditions of the physical world. They have no senses of the kind which man possesses. Their knowledge is like man's; only they have not acquired it through the gateway of the senses, but through a kind of ascent, or mounting-up of their ideas and other soul-experiences out of the depths of their being. Their inner life is, as it were, at rest within them, and they draw it up out of the depths of their souls, as man from the depths of his soul draws up his memory-pictures.

In this way man becomes acquainted with beings who have become within the supersensible world that which he may become within the physical world. Owing to this, these beings are a stage higher than man in the order of the universe, although they may be said to be, in the manner indicated, of the same nature as he. They constitute a kingdom above man, a hierarchy superior to him in the scale of beings. Notwithstanding their similarity to man, their etheric body is different from his. Whereas man is woven into the supersensible life-body of the earth through the sympathies and antipathies of his etheric body, these beings are not earth-bound in the life of their soul.

If man observes what these beings experience through their etheric bodies, he finds that their experiences are similar to those of his own soul. They have thinking power; they have feelings and a will. But through their etheric body they develop something which man can only develop through the physical body. Through their etheric body they arrive at a consciousness of their own being, although man would not be able to know anything about a supersensible being unless he carried up into supersensible worlds the forces which he acquires in the physical body.

Clairvoyant consciousness learns to know these beings through developing a faculty for observing them by the help of the human etheric body. This clairvoyant consciousness lifts the human soul up into the world in which these beings have their field of activity and their abode. Not till the soul experiences itself in that world, do pictures or conceptions arise in its consciousness which bring about knowledge of these beings. For these beings do not interpose directly in the physical world, nor therefore in man's physical body. They are not present in the experiences which may be made through that body. They are spiritual, supersensible beings, who do not, so to say, set foot in the physical world.

If man does not respect the boundary between the physical world and supersensible worlds, it may happen that he drags into his physical consciousness supersensible images which are not the true expression of these beings. These images arise through experiencing the Luciferic and Ahrimanic beings, who though of like nature to the supersensible beings just described, are contrasted with them through having transferred their field of activity and their abodes to the world which man perceives as the physical world.

When man with clairvoyant consciousness contemplates the Luciferic and Ahrimanic beings from the supersensible world, after having through his experience with the Guardian of the Threshold, learned the right way to observe the boundary between that world and physical existence, he learns to know these beings in their reality, and to distinguish them from those other spiritual beings who have remained in the sphere of action adapted to their nature. It is from this standpoint that spiritual science must portray the Luciferic and Ahrimanic beings.

It then appears that the field of activity adapted to the Luciferic beings is not the physical but, in a certain respect, the elemental world. When something penetrates into the human soul which rises as though out of the waves of that world like pictures, and when these pictures work with a vivifying effect on man's etheric body, without assuming an illusive existence in the soul, then the Luciferic essence may be present in these images, without its activity transgressing against the order of the universe. In this case the Luciferic nature has the effect of emancipation upon the human soul, raising it above mere entanglement in the physical world. But when the human soul draws into the physical body the life which it should only develop in the elemental world, when it allows feeling within the physical body to be influenced by sympathies and antipathies which should only hold sway in the etheric body, then the Luciferic nature gains through that soul an influence which is opposed to the general order of the universe. This influence is always present when in the sympathies and antipathies of the physical world, something is working besides that love which is based on sympathy with the life of another being present in that world. Such a being may be loved because it comes before the one loving it endowed with certain qualities; in this case there is no admixture of a Luciferic element with the love. Love which has its basis in those qualities in the beloved being which are manifest in physical existence, keeps clear of Luciferic interference. But love, the source of which is not thus in the beloved being, but in the one loving it, is prone to the Luciferic influence. A being loved because it has qualities to which, as lovers, we incline by nature is loved with that part of the soul which is accessible to the Luciferic element.

We should therefore never say that the Luciferic element is bad under all circumstances, for events and beings of supersensible worlds must be loved by the human soul in the manner of the Luciferic element. The order of the universe is not transgressed until the kind of love with which man ought to feel himself drawn to the supersensible is directed to physical things. Love for the supersensible rightly calls forth in the one loving it an enhanced feeling of self; love which in the physical world is sought for the sake of such an enhanced feeling of self is equivalent to a Luciferic temptation. Love of the spiritual when it is sought for the sake of the self has the effect of emancipation; but love for the physical when it is sought on account of the self has not this effect, but, through the gratification gained by its means, only puts the self in fetters.

The Ahrimanic beings make themselves felt in the thinking soul just as the Luciferic beings affect the feeling soul. The former chain thought to the physical world. They turn it away from the fact that thoughts of any kind are only of importance when they assert themselves as part of the great thought-order of the world which cannot be found within physical existence. In the world into which the human life of the soul is woven, the Ahrimanic element must exist as a necessary counterbalance to the Luciferic. Without the Luciferic element, the soul would dream away its life in observation of physical existence, and feel no impulse to rise above it. Without the counter-effect of the Ahrimanic element, the soul would fall a victim to the Luciferic influence; it would underrate the importance of the physical world, in spite of the fact that some of its necessary conditions of existence are in that world. It would not wish to have anything to do with the physical world. The Ahrimanic element has the right degree of importance in the human soul when it leads to a way of living in the physical world which is suitable to that world; when we take it for what it is, and are able to dispense with everything in it which in its nature must be transitory. It is quite impossible to say that a person could avoid falling a victim to the Luciferic and Ahrimanic elements by rooting them out of himself. It is, for instance, possible that if the Luciferic element in him were rooted out, his soul would no longer aspire to the supersensible; or, if the Ahrimanic element were eradicated, that he might not any more realise the full importance of the physical world: the right relation to one of these elements is arrived at when the proper counterpoise to it is provided in the other. All harmful effects from these cosmic beings proceed entirely from one of them becoming the unlimited master of the situation, whatever it may be, and from not being brought into the right harmony through the opposite force.

XII

Concerning Spiritual Cosmic Beings

WHEN clairvoyant consciousness comes to life in the elemental world, it finds beings there who are able to develop a life in that world which man only acquires within the physical world. These beings do not feel their self—their ego—as man feels his in the physical world; they permeate that self with their will much more than man does his; they will their own existence as it were, and feel their existence as something which they give to themselves through their will. On the other hand, with regard to their thinking, they have not the feeling that they are creating their thoughts, as man creates his; they feel all their thoughts as inspirations, as something which is not in them but in the universe, and which is streaming out of the universe into their being. Thus in these beings no doubt can ever arise but that their thoughts are the reflection of the thought-order poured forth into the universe. They do not think their own thoughts, but cosmic thoughts. With their activity of thought they live in cosmic thoughts; but they will their existence. Their life of feeling is shaped in accordance with this will and thought of theirs. They feel themselves to be a link in the whole cosmic system; and they feel the necessity of willing their existence in a manner corresponding to that system.

When the clairvoyant soul grows familiar with the world inhabited by these beings, it comes naturally to an idea of its own thinking, feeling, and willing. These faculties of the human soul could not be unfolded within the elemental world in man's etheric body. Human will would remain only a weak, dreamlike faculty in the elemental world, human thought merely an indistinct, fleeting world of ideas. No feeling of the ego would come into existence there at all. For all these things it is necessary for man to be invested with a physical body.

When the clairvoyant human soul ascends from the elemental world into the spiritual world proper, it experiences itself in conditions which diverge still further than do elemental conditions from those of the physical world. In the elemental world there is still much that is reminiscent of the physical world; but in the spiritual world man confronts entirely new conditions. He can do nothing there if he has only the ideas which are to be gained in the physical world. All the same, man's inner life as a human soul in the physical world must be so strengthened that he will bring over from that world into the spiritual world that which makes a sojourn there possible. If such a strengthened life of the soul were not brought into the spiritual world, man would simply lapse into unconsciousness there. He could only be present there in the same sort of way in which a plant is present in the physical world. We have, as human souls, to bring with us into the spiritual world all those things not really existing in the physical world but manifesting themselves there nevertheless as if they were existent. We must be able to form conceptions in the physical world, which, though prompted by that world, do not directly correspond to any thing or occurrence in it. Every delineation of things in the physical world, or description of physical occurrences, is meaningless in the spiritual world. What may be perceived with the senses, or expressed in conceptions applicable in the physical world, does not exist in the spiritual world. On entering the latter, everything to which physical ideas can be applied must, so to speak, be left behind. But ideas which have been so formed in the physical world that they do not correspond to any physical thing or process, are still present in the soul when it enters the spiritual world. Naturally some of these ideas may have been formed erroneously. If these are present in the consciousness on its entering the spiritual world, by their very being they prove themselves as not belonging to that world. They act in such a way as to impress on the soul the urgency of returning to the physical world or the elemental world, in order to exchange these erroneous ideas for the right ones. But when the soul brings correct ideas into the spiritual world, what is related to them in that world presses to meet them; the soul finds there beings who in their whole inner substance are essentially of the same nature as thoughts. These beings have a body, which may be called a thought-body. In this body they experience themselves as independent beings, just as man experiences himself independently within the physical world.

Now amongst the conceptions acquired by man, there are certain thoughts saturated with feelings which are adapted to strengthen the life of the soul in such a way that it is able to receive an impression from the beings of the spiritual world. When the feeling of self-surrender, such as must be developed for the faculty of transformation in the elemental world, becomes so much intensified that in that surrender the being into which we are transformed is felt not merely as sympathetic or antipathetic, but can live again in its own special way in the soul surrendered to it, then the faculty of perception of the spiritual world is coming into existence. Then one spiritual beings speaks, as it were, in one way to the soul, another in another way; and a spiritual intercourse ensues, which consists in a language of thoughts. We experience thoughts; but we know that we are experiencing beings in these thoughts. To live in beings who do not merely express themselves in thoughts, but are actually present in those thoughts with their individuality, is to live with the soul in the spiritual world.

With regard, however, to the beings of the elemental world, the soul has the feeling that they have the cosmic thoughts flowing into their own individual beings, and that they will their own existence in conformity with this universal thought streaming into them.

But with regard to the beings who need not descend to the elemental world to gain that which man can only gain in the physical world, and who already attain that stage of existence in the spiritual world, the human soul has the feeling that they consist wholly of thought substance; that not only do the cosmic thoughts flow into them, but that the beings themselves actually live in that weaving of thought with their individuality. They entirely allow the cosmic thoughts to think themselves within them in a living way. Their life consists in the apprehension of this cosmic language of thought, and their willing consists in their being able to express themselves in thought. This thought-existence of theirs reacts vitally upon the universe, for thoughts which are beings converse with other thoughts which are also beings.

Man's life of thought is the reflection of this spiritual life of thought-beings. During the period through which the human soul passes between death and re-birth, it is woven into this life of thought-beings, just as it is woven into physical existence between birth and death. When the soul enters physical existence through birth, or rather through conception, the permanent thought-entity of the soul works in a shaping and inspiring way on the fate of that soul. In human destiny what has remained of the soul from the earth-lives preceding the present one, works in the same way as pure living thought-beings work in the universe.

When clairvoyant consciousness enters this spiritual world of living thought-beings, it feels itself to be in a completely new relationship towards the physical world. The latter confronts it in the spiritual world as another world, just as in the physical world the spiritual world appears as another one. But to spiritual sight the physical world has lost everything which can be perceived of it within physical existence. All those qualities seem to have vanished which are grasped with the senses, or the intellect which is bound up with the senses. On the other hand, it is obvious from the standpoint of the spiritual world that the true, original nature of the physical world is itself spiritual. To the soul's gaze, looking from the spiritual world, there appear instead of the previous physical world, spiritual beings unfolding their activities in such a way that through the converging of those activities that world comes into being which, looked at through the senses, is the very world that man has before him in his own physical existence. Seen from the spiritual world, the qualities, forces, materials, etc., of the physical world disappear as such, and are revealed as mere semblance. From the spiritual world man sees only beings, and in them lies true reality.

Similarly from the elemental world, when beheld from the spiritual world, there vanishes everything which is not actual being. And the soul feels that in this world too, it has to do with beings who, by letting their activities converge, cause an existence to become manifest which through the organs of sympathy and antipathy appears as elemental.

The essential part of projecting one's life into supersensible worlds consists in the fact that beings take the place of the conditions and qualities which the consciousness has around it in the physical world. The supersensible world reveals itself ultimately as a world of beings, and whatever exists in addition to those beings is the expression of their actions. Indeed, both the physical world and the elemental world appear as the deeds of spiritual beings.

XIII

The First Beginnings of Man's Physical Body

EARLIER in this book mention was made of a
Moon and Sun condition, preceding the Earth
condition, and only in that Moon period do there
still appear to clairvoyant consciousness impressions
which are reminiscent of the impressions of earth-
life. Such impressions are no longer to be gained
when clairvoyant sight is directed to the still further
distant past of the earth's Sun condition. The
latter is revealed wholly as a world of beings and the
actions of those beings. In order to get an impression of this Sun period, it is necessary to keep at a
distance all ideas of the earth's mineral and plant
life. For such ideas only have a meaning with
regard to earlier conditions of the earth period;
and, those of them which concern plant-life, to the
long-past Moon period. To the earth's ancient Sun
condition conceptions lead which may be prompted
by the animal and human kingdoms of nature—
conceptions, however, which do not merely portray
what the senses disclose about the inhabitants of
these kingdoms.

Now the clairvoyant consciousness of man finds
within the etheric body active forces which form
themselves into pictures of such a kind that they

bring to expression the way in which the etheric body received, through the actions of spiritual beings during the ancient Sun period, its first beginning in the cosmic order of things. This beginning may be traced in its further development through the Moon and Earth periods. We find that in the course of these it was transformed, and through this transformation became what is now seen to be the active etheric body of man.

In order to understand the physical body of man, we require, however, a different activity of human consciousness. At first it appears as an outer counterpart of the etheric body. But close observation shows that man in the sense-world could never arrive at a complete development of his being, unless the physical body were something more than merely a physical manifestation of the etheric body. If this were so, definite willing, feeling, and thinking would take place in man, but they could not be so synthetised that the consciousness which expresses itself as an ego-experience could arise in the human soul. This becomes specially evident when the consciousness develops the quality of clairvoyance. Man's ego-experience can at first only take place in the physical world, when he is invested with his physical body. Thence he is able to take his experience into the elemental and spiritual worlds and interpenetrate his etheric and astral bodies with it. For man has an etheric and an astral body in which the ego-experience does not at first arise. Only in his physical body can that experience take place. Now if the human physical body is looked at from the spiritual world, it turns out that there is something in it, belonging to it intrinsically, which even from the spiritual world is not fully disclosed in its reality. If the consciousness enters the spiritual world in a clairvoyant capacity, the soul grows familiar with the world of thought-reality; but the ego experience, which through an adequate strengthening of soul-force may be carried into that world, is not woven simply out of universal thoughts; it does not yet feel in the world of cosmic thoughts anything in that environment which is equal to its own being. In order to feel this, the soul must advance still further into the supersensible. It must come to experiences in which it is abandoned even by thoughts, so that all physical experiences and all experiences also of thinking, feeling, and willing are, as it were, left behind it on its journey into the supersensible. Then for the first time does it feel itself one with a reality which so underlies the universe that it takes precedence of everything which man, as a physical, etheric, and astral being, is able to observe. Man then feels himself in a still higher sphere than the spiritual world so far known to him. We will call this world in which only the ego can experience itself, the super-spiritual world. From it even the region of thought-reality seems an outer world. When clairvoyant consciousness is transferred to this super-spiritual world, it goes through an experience which may be described and characterised somewhat as follows, by tracing the path followed by clairvoyant consciousness through its various stages.

86

When the soul feels itself in its etheric body, and elemental events and beings are its environment, it knows it is outside the physical body; but that physical body still exists as an entity, although when seen from without it appears transformed. To spiritual sight a part of it becomes detached, and is manifest as the expression of the deeds of spiritual beings who have been active from the beginnings of the earth's existence up to the present time. Another detached part appears as the expression of something which was already in existence during the ancient Moon condition of the earth. This state of things continues as long as the consciousness is only experiencing itself in the elemental world. In that world the consciousness is able to become aware of the way in which man was constituted as a physical being during the ancient Moon period.

When the consciousness enters the spiritual world, another part of the physical body becomes detached. It is the part which was formed during the Moon period by the deeds of spiritual beings. But another part is left behind. It is that which existed during the Sun condition of the earth as man's physical entity at that period. But even of this physical entity something is left behind, when, from the standpoint of the spiritual world, everything is taken into account which happened during the Sun period through the deeds of spiritual beings.

What is then left behind is first revealed as the action of spiritual beings when the consciousness reaches the super-spiritual world. It is revealed as already existent at the beginning of the Sun period, and we have to go back to a condition of the earth before its Sun period. In my book *Occult Science*, I endeavoured to vindicate the use of the term Saturn period for this condition of the earth's existence. In this sense the earth was Saturn before it became Sun. And during that Saturn period the first beginning of the physical human body came into existence out of the cosmic world-process through the deeds of spiritual beings. That beginning was afterwards so transformed during the succeeding Sun, Moon, and Earth periods by the further actions of other spiritual beings that the present physical human body became what it now is.

XIV

Concerning Man's True Ego

WHEN the soul experiences itself in its astral body and has living thought-beings as its environment, it knows itself to be outside both the physical and etheric bodies. But it also feels that its thinking, feeling, and willing belong but to a limited sphere of the universe, whereas in virtue of its own original nature it should embrace much more than is allotted to it in that sphere. The soul that has become clairvoyant may say to itself within the spiritual world: " In the physical world I am confined to what my physical body allows me to observe; in the elemental world I am limited by my etheric body; in the spiritual world I am restricted by finding myself, as it were, upon an island in the universe and by feeling my spiritual existence bounded by the shores of that island. Beyond them is a world which I should be able to perceive if I were to work my way through the veil which is woven before the eyes of my spirit by the actions of living thought-beings." Now the soul is indeed able to work its way through this veil, if it continues to develop further and further the faculty of self-surrender which is already necessary for its life in the elemental world. It is under the necessity of still further strengthening the forces which accrue to it from experience in the physical world, in order to be guarded in supersensible worlds from having its consciousness deadened, clouded, or even annihilated. In the physical world the soul, in order to experience thoughts within itself, has need only of the strength naturally allotted to it apart from its own inner work. In the elemental world thoughts, which immediately on arising fall into oblivion, are softened down to dreamlike experience, i.e. do not come into the consciousness at all, unless the soul, before entering this world, has worked on the strengthening of its inner life. For this purpose it must specially strengthen the will-power, for in the elemental world a thought is no longer merely a thought; it has an inner activity, or life of its own. It has to be held fast by the will if it is not to leave the circle of the consciousness. In the spiritual world thoughts are completely in-dependent living beings. If they are to remain in the consciousness, the soul must be so strengthened that it develops within itself and of itself the force which the physical body develops for it in the physical world, and which in the elemental world is developed by the sympathies and antipathies of the etheric body. It must forgo all this assistance in the spiritual world. There the experiences of the physical world and the elemental world are only present to the soul as memories. And the soul itself is beyond those two worlds. Around it is the spiritual world. This world at first makes no impression upon the astral body. The soul has to learn to live by itself on its own memories. The content of its consciousness is at first merely this: " I have existed, and now I am confronting nothingness." But when the memories come from such soul-experiences as are not merely reproductions of physical or elemental occurrences, but represent free thought-experiences induced by those occurrences, there begins in the soul an exchange of thought between the memories and the supposed nothingness of the spiritual environment. And that which arises as the result of that intercourse becomes a world of conceptions in the consciousness of the astral body. The strength which is needful for the soul at this point of its development is such as will make it capable of standing on the shore of the only world hitherto known to it, and of enduring the facing of supposed nothingness. This supposed nothingness is at first an absolutely real nothingness to the soul. Yet the soul still has, so to speak, behind it the world of its memories. It can, as it were, take a firm grip of them. It can live in them. And the more it lives in them, the more it strengthens the forces of the astral body. With this strengthening begins the intercourse between its past existence and the beings of the spiritual world. During this intercourse the soul learns to feel itself as an astral being. To use an expression in keeping with ancient traditions, we may say, " The human soul experiences itself as an astral being within the cosmic Word." By the cosmic Word are here meant the thought-deeds of living thought-beings, which are enacted in the spiritual world like a living discourse of spirits; but in such a way that these discourses

91

exactly correspond in the spiritual world to deeds in the physical world.

If the soul now wishes to step over into the super-spiritual world, it must efface, by its own will, its memories of the physical and elemental worlds. It can only do this when it has gained the certainty, from the spirit discourse, that it will not wholly lose its existence if it effaces everything in itself which so far the consciousness of that existence has given it. The soul must actually place itself at the edge of a spiritual abyss and there make an act of will to forget its willing, feeling, and thinking. It must consciously renounce its past. The resolution that has to be taken at this point may be called a bringing about of complete sleep of the consciousness by one's own will, not by conditions of the physical or etheric body. Only this resolution must not be thought of as having for its object a return, after an interval of unconsciousness, to the same consciousness that was previously there, but as if that consciousness, by means of the resolution, really plunges into forgetfulness by its own act of will. It must be borne in mind that this process is not possible in either the physical or the elemental world, but only in the spiritual world. In the physical world the annihilation which appears as death is possible; in the elemental world there is no death. Man, in so far as he belongs to the elemental world, cannot die, he can only be transformed into another being. In the spiritual world, however, no positive transformation, in the strict sense of the word, is possible; for into whatever a human being may change, his past experience is revealed in the spiritual world as his own conscious existence. If this memory existence is to disappear within the spiritual world, it must be because the soul itself, by an act of will, has caused it to sink into oblivion. Clairvoyant consciousness is able to perform such an act of will when it has won the necessary inner strength. If it arrives at this, there emerges from the forgetfulness it has itself brought about the true being of the ego. The super-spiritual environment gives the human soul the knowledge of that true ego. Just as clairvoyant consciousness can experience itself in the etheric and astral bodies, so too can it experience itself in the true ego.

This true ego is not created by clairvoyance; it exists in the depths of every human soul. Clairvoyant consciousness simply experiences consciously a fact appertaining to the nature of every human soul, of which it is not conscious.

After physical death man gradually lives himself into the spiritual environment. At first his being emerges into it with memories of the physical world. Then, although he has not the assistance of his physical body, he can nevertheless live consciously in those memories, because the living thought-beings corresponding to them incorporate themselves into the memories, so that the latter no longer have the merely shadowy existence peculiar to them in the physical world. And at a definite point of time between death and re-birth, the living thought-beings of the spiritual environment exert such a strong influence that, without any act of will, the oblivion which has been described is brought about. And at that moment life emerges in the true ego. Clairvoyant consciousness, by strengthening the life of the soul, brings about as a free action of the spirit that which is, so to speak, a natural occurrence between death and re-birth. Nevertheless, memory of previous earth-lives can never arise within physical experience, unless the thoughts have, during those earth-lives, been directed to the spiritual world. It is always necessary first to have known of a thing in order that a clearly recognisable remembrance of it may arise later. Therefore we must, during one earth-life, gain knowledge of ourselves as spiritual beings if we are to be justified in expecting that in our next earthly existence we shall be able to remember a former one.

Yet this knowledge need not necessarily be gained through clairvoyance. When a person acquires a direct knowledge of the spiritual world through clairvoyance, there may arise in his soul, during the earth-lives following the one in which he gained that knowledge, a memory of the former one, in the same way in which the memory of a personal experience presents itself in physical existence. In the case, however, of one who penetrates into spiritual science with true comprehension, though without clairvoyance, the memory will occur in such a form that it may be compared with the remembrance in physical existence of an event of which he has only heard a description.

94

XV

Summary of Part of the Foregoing

MAN bears within him a true ego, which belongs to a super-spiritual world. In the physical world this true ego is, as it were, concealed by the experiences of thinking, feeling, and willing. Even in the spiritual world man only becomes aware of his true ego when he effaces in himself the memories of everything which he is able to experience through his thinking, feeling, and willing. The knowledge of the true ego emerges out of forgetfulness of what is experienced in the physical world, the elemental world, and the spiritual world.

The human physical body is revealed in its true nature when the soul beholds it from the super-spiritual world. Then it becomes evident that that body first took its rise out of the universal cosmic process during a Saturn period which preceded the Sun period of the earth. Subsequently, during the Sun, Moon, and Earth periods, it developed into what the human physical body is at present.

In accordance with the foregoing, man's collective being may be expressed in tabular form as follows:

I. *The physical body in the environment of the physical world.* By its means man recognises himself as an independent individual being or ego. This physical body was formed, at its first beginning, from the universal cosmic essence during a long-past Saturn period of the earth, and through its development during four planetary metamorphoses of the earth has become what it now is.

II. *The subtle, etheric body in the elemental environment.* By its means man recognises himself as a member of the earth's elemental or life body. This body was formed, at its first beginning, from the universal cosmic essence during a long-past Sun period of the earth, and through its development during three planetary metamorphoses of the earth has become what it now is.

III. *The astral body in a spiritual environment.* Through it man is a member of a spiritual world. In it is situated man's other self which realises itself in repeated earth-lives.

IV. *The true ego in a super-spiritual environment.* In this man finds himself as a spiritual being, even when all experiences of the physical, elemental, and spiritual worlds, and therefore all experiences of the senses and of thinking, feeling, and willing, sink into oblivion.

XVI

Remarks on the Connection of what is described in this Book with the Accounts given in my Books Theosophy *and* Occult Science

NAMES which are to express the experiences of the human soul in the elemental and spiritual worlds must be adapted to the special characteristics of those experiences. In giving such names it will have to be borne in mind that even in the elemental world experience runs its course in quite a different way from that in which it does in the physical world. Experience in the elemental world is due to the soul's .capacity for transformation and to its observation of sympathies and antipathies. The terminology will necessarily assume something of the changeful character of such experiences. It cannot be as fixed and rigid as it must be with regard to the physical world. One who does not keep in view this fact, arising out of the nature of the case, may easily find a contradiction between the terminology used in this book and that in *Theosophy* and *Occult Science*. The contradiction disappears when it is remembered that in the two latter works the names are so chosen that they characterise those experiences which the soul has during its complete development between birth (conception) and death on the one hand, and between death and re-birth on the other. In this book, however, the names are given with reference to the experiences of clairvoyant consciousness when it enters the elemental world and the spiritual spheres.

It is seen from *Theosophy* and *Occult Science* that soon after the detachment of the physical body from the soul at death, there is also detached from the soul that which in this book is called the etheric body. The soul then lives for a while in the entity which is here called the astral body. The etheric body, after being detached from the soul, is transformed within the elemental world. It passes into the beings forming that world. When this transformation of the etheric body takes place, the soul which had lived in it is no longer there. The soul, however, experiences as its outer world after death the processes of the elemental world. This experience of the elemental world "from without" is described in *Theosophy* and *Occult Science* as the passage of the soul through the "soul-world." It must therefore be realised that this soul-world is identical with that which, from the standpoint of clairvoyant consciousness, is in this book called the elemental world.

When the soul in the interval between death and re-birth—as described in *Theosophy*—becomes detached from its astral body, it goes on living in the entity which is here called the true ego. The astral body then experiences by itself, the soul being no longer with it, that which has been described above as oblivion. It plunges, so to speak, into a world in which there is nothing which can be observed with the senses, or experienced in the way in which will, feeling and thought, as man develops them in his physical body, experience things. This world is experienced as its outer world by the soul which continues to exist in the true ego. If it is desirable to characterise the experience in this outer world, it can be done in the same way in which it is described in *Theosophy* and *Occult Science*, as the passing through the " spirit region." The soul, experiencing itself in the true ego, has around it within the spiritual world that which has been formed in it as soul-experiences during physical existence. Within the world above described as that of living thought-beings, the soul finds between death and re-birth all that it has experienced in its inner being during physical existence through its sense perceptions and its thinking, feeling, and willing.

COSIMO is a specialty publisher of books and publications that inspire, inform and engage readers. Our mission is to offer unique books to niche audiences around the world.

COSIMO CLASSICS offers a collection of distinctive titles by the great authors and thinkers throughout the ages. At **COSIMO CLASSICS** timeless classics find a new life as affordable books, covering a variety of subjects including: *Biographies, Business, History, Mythology, Personal Development, Philosophy, Religion and Spirituality*, and much more!

COSIMO-on-DEMAND publishes books and publications for innovative authors, non-profit organizations and businesses. **COSIMO-on-DEMAND** specializes in bringing books back into print, publishing new books quickly and effectively, and making these publications available to readers around the world.

COSIMO REPORTS publishes public reports that affect your world: from global trends to the economy, and from health to geo-politics.

FOR MORE INFORMATION CONTACT US AT
INFO@COSIMOBOOKS.COM

If you are a book-lover interested in our current catalog of books.

If you are an author who wants to get published

If you represent an organization or business seeking to reach your members, donors or customers with your own books and publications

**COSIMO BOOKS ARE ALWAYS
AVAILABLE AT ONLINE BOOKSTORES**

VISIT COSIMOBOOKS.COM
BE INSPIRED, BE INFORMED

Printed in the United States
99568LV00004B/311/A

9 781602 060524